OUTDOOR SCIENCE

OUTDOOR SCIENCE

30 AWESOME STEM EXPERIMENTS TO TRY AT HOME

Button
BOOKS

LAURA MINTER & TIA WILLIAMS

Contents

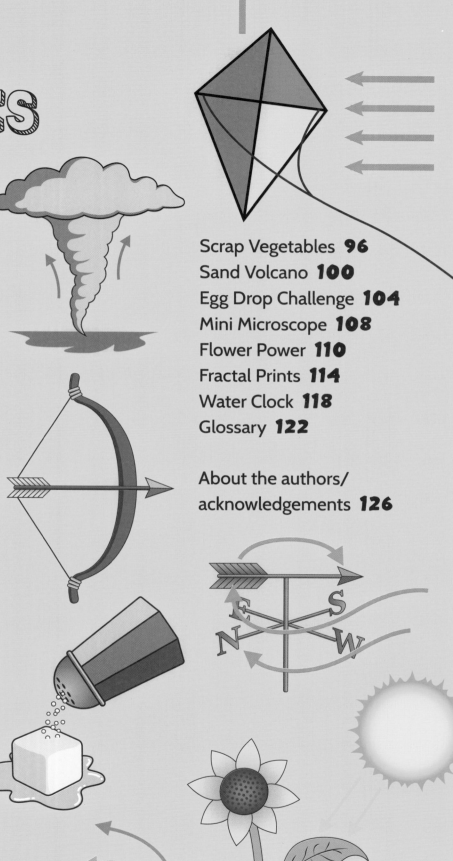

Introduction

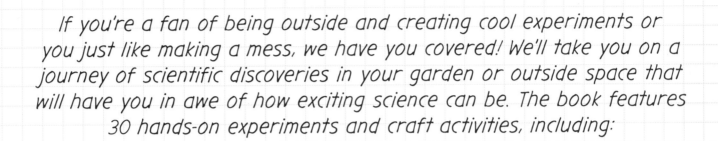

If you're a fan of being outside and creating cool experiments or you just like making a mess, we have you covered! We'll take you on a journey of scientific discoveries in your garden or outside space that will have you in awe of how exciting science can be. The book features 30 hands-on experiments and craft activities, including:

☑ **Mud bombs to learn about chemical reactions**

☑ **Stick slingshot to learn about potential and kinetic energy**

☑ **Spectroscope to learn about light reflection and diffraction**

☑ **Solar still to learn about how water acts and the water cycle**

This book is designed to encourage you to ask questions, to try and figure out why certain things happen, and to be curious about the natural world. Exploring outside and finding out about things like plant growth, weather patterns, habitats, stars, and chemical reactions helps us to learn things in a much more exciting and memorable way. Plus experimenting in the real world is a lot more fun than just reading about it in a textbook at school!

This book is filled with tons of inspiring ideas that you can try again and again. There are hands-on learning experiences that will allow you to observe natural phenomena, conduct experiments, and interact with the environment. There are over 30 projects that are easy to follow with step-by-step instructions and accompanying photographs to help you along the way. All the projects are suitable for beginners.

WHY IS SCIENCE SO IMPORTANT?

Science is like a superpower! Everything we know about the world, our existence in it, where we came from and where we are going—it is all thanks to the work of scientists.

Science helps us to answer loads of really cool questions, like why are flowers colorful, what are clouds, and why are bubbles round? Encouraging young minds to be curious is a great way to get thinking about things on a deeper level. If, instead of playing on screens for an hour we decided to head outside armed with a magnifying glass and a specimen jar, just imagine how much more we could learn.

Science makes our lives and the world we live in more exciting. So if you want to join in this journey of discovery, get outside, and conduct loads of cool experiments then you have come to the right place!

Getting Started

The important thing to note here is that you do not need tons of materials to work through the projects in this book. A lot of the materials you'll already have in your kitchen cupboard or craft stocks. Below is an idea of some of the materials you will find useful for the projects in the book. Please note that since scissors are used in nearly all of the projects they do not appear in individual project lists. Children may need help with some of the activities that use them.

THE RECYCLING BIN
- ☑ Plastic bottles
- ☑ Cardboard boxes and tubes
- ☑ Glass jars of various sizes
- ☑ Old pots

FOOD ITEMS
- ☑ Cornstarch
- ☑ Food coloring
- ☑ Bicarbonate of soda
- ☑ Vinegar

OTHER ITEMS
- ☑ Old mixing bowls, spoons, and cups
- ☑ Sand

CRAFT ESSENTIALS
- ☑ Paint
- ☑ Tissue paper
- ☑ Air-dry clay
- ☑ Crayons
- ☑ Glue (PVA and stronger craft glue)
- ☑ Sticky back plastic
- ☑ Colorful card and paper

SAFE SCIENCE

The projects in this book are designed to be safe to do with a little adult supervision. However, it is still important to bear in mind that with any science experiment a degree of caution is needed. Treat substances you haven't handled before with care and wear safety goggles and gloves where appropriate. The experiment involving flames will need an adult to help. Any specific areas of caution are flagged up in the relevant sections of the book.

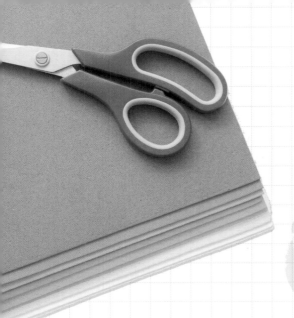

Rainbow Machine

Learn about the color spectrum and how rainbows are formed with this spectroscope, which splits light into different wavelengths, creating beautiful rainbow colors.

YOU WILL NEED

- ☑ An old CD
- ☑ A cardboard tube (paper-towel length)
- ☑ Scrap of card
- ☑ Pencil
- ☑ Paint
- ☑ Paintbrush
- ☑ Masking tape
- ☑ Sharp knife

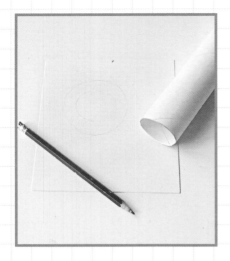

1 Place one end of the cardboard tube on the card and draw around it. Draw another rough circle about ½in (1cm) bigger around the first circle.

2 Cut around the outer circle. Then cut slits from the outer to the inner circle to make tabs.

3 Cut a slit (about 1½ x ½in/4 x 1cm) in the center of the circle. Fold in the tabs, then tape it onto the end of the cardboard tube. Paint and decorate the cardboard tube however you like.

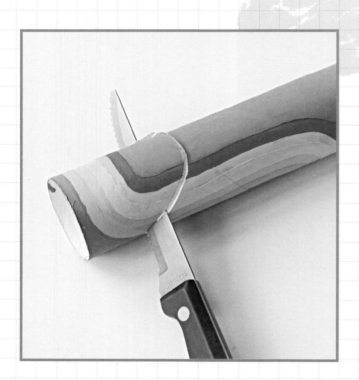

4 Measure about 2½in (6cm) from the open end of the cardboard tube and ask an adult to cut a slit diagonally (at a 45 degree angle) halfway into the tube.

5 Just behind the slit, measure and cut a small rectangle measuring about 1 x ½in (3 x 1cm) for a peep-hole. Insert the CD into the slit, with the reflective side up.

6 Head outside into a nice bright spot. Point the top of the spectroscope at an angle to the sky, being careful not to point it directly at the sun. Look through the peephole behind the CD. What can you see? You should see a rainbow in the tube! You will probably have to move the tube around a little to get the best angle to be able to see it.

SCIENCE MADE SIMPLE

Sunlight is made up of lots of colors that have different **WAVELENGTHS**. The **REFLECTIVE** surface of the CD is made up of spirals of raised lines. When light hits these lines it spreads out—the light **DIFFRACTS**. The raised lines make the reflected light travel in different directions. Some of the rays of light combine to give the different colors. This diffracted light is reflected into the tube. The pattern of colors produced is called a **SPECTRUM**.

Air and Smoke Cannon

Shoot air at paper-cup towers, navigate a pompom across a chalk maze, make smoke rings, fire pompoms at targets, and learn about vortexes at the same time!

YOU WILL NEED
- ☑ Plastic bottle
- ☑ Balloon
- ☑ Craft tape
- ☑ Colored chalks
- ☑ Pompoms
- ☑ 6 paper cups
- ☑ Incense stick or long match

1 Ask a grown-up to cut the plastic bottle in half. Discard the bottom bit and the lid. Make sure there are no sharp edges and trim to smooth if necessary. Tie the end of the balloon (without blowing it up), then cut off the top, about a quarter of the way in.

2 Stretch the balloon over the open end of the bottle, overlapping by about 1in (2.5cm). Use tape to hold the balloon in place.

3 First, test the cannon out. Hold the bottle with the neck pointing at your face. Pull back on the balloon and release it. You should get a strong puff of air in your face. It will probably make you jump!

4 Line up a stack of cups. Can you use the air cannon to knock them over with just the power of air?

5 Try drawing a little path in chalk on pavement and see if you can direct a pompom from A to B with your air cannon. If it crosses the line you have to start again. Challenge your friends and time yourselves to see who can get there fastest. You could also try loading the pompoms into the bottle and firing them at a chalk target.

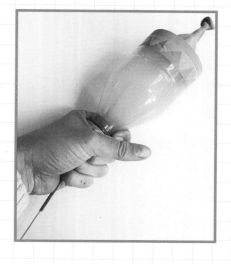

6 Use the cannon to create smoke rings. This works best if it is dark outside or against a dark background, and if there is no breeze. Ask an adult to light an incense stick. Hold it carefully with the lit end inside the bottle, being careful to ensure it doesn't touch the plastic. Try to block the bottle neck so that the smoke doesn't escape.

7 After a few minutes, the bottle should be filled with smoke. Remove the incense and cover the mouth of the bottle to stop the smoke escaping.

8 Uncover the mouth of the bottle, then with the palm of your hand tap the balloon end of the bottle. You should see a ring of smoke come out of the bottle! Keep tapping. You should be able to make at least 20 smoke rings before it empties. It may take a bit of practice working out the optimum amount of force to apply to get the best smoke ring.

SCIENCE MADE SIMPLE

When you pull back the balloon on your air cannon, you are drawing air into the bottle through the neck. When you let go, that air is quickly forced out of the neck because there is less space in the bottle. This creates a **VORTEX** of air or smoke. A vortex is a mass of spiraling air or water. You can only feel it with the air cannon, but with the smoke rings you can see the swirling smoke as it comes out of the bottle.

Can you think of any other vortexes that you've seen before? In nature you can see them in the form of tornados (rotating columns of air) and whirlpools (circular currents in seas and rivers). When you pull the plug in a bath you will notice the water whooshing around the drain in a vortex.

Spiraling air is pushed upward in a tornado.

Bubble Science

Make your own bubbles and wands while learning about what bubbles are and how they are formed. The guar gum is optional, but it improves elasticity and makes them last a bit longer. You can find it from health food stores or order online.

YOU WILL NEED

- ☑ 1 tbsp glycerin
- ☑ 1¾fl oz (50ml) good-quality dishwashing liquid
- ☑ 10fl oz (300ml) hot water
- ☑ ¼ tsp guar gum (optional)
- ☑ About 8 drinking paper straws
- ☑ Strong glue

Tip

You can also make popsicle wands, which will make bigger bubbles! Arrange the popsicle sticks into whatever shape you like. When you are happy with your design, glue the sticks together and paint in colors of your choice.

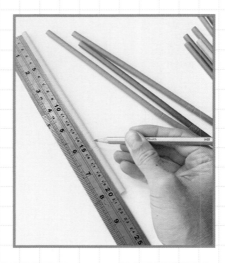

1 Pour 10fl oz (300ml) of hot water into a bowl and stir in the glycerin and guar gum, then gently mix in the dishwashing liquid. Leave the mixture to sit overnight to allow the ingredients to stabilize.

2 While you're waiting, make some bubble wands. To make a star straw wand, measure and mark seven of the straws all the way along the lengths at ½in (1cm) intervals.

3 Cut the straws up to create lots of little beads.

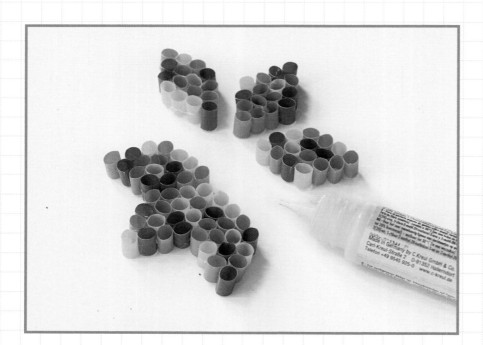

4 Glue four of the straw beads together in a row. Then glue three more beads alongside them, then two beads, and then one bead to create a triangle. Repeat on the other side to turn the triangle into a diamond. See the step image to guide you. Make six diamonds in this way, then glue all of them together to create a star.

5 Glue a long straw onto the bottom for a handle. Glue more straw beads together however you would like to create different shaped wands.

6 When you are ready, pour a little bubble mix into a dish and dip the wands in the solution to make your bubbles. Can you see all the colors in the bubbles? Why do you think each bubble is so perfectly round?

SCIENCE MADE SIMPLE

BUBBLES are delicate layers of soap and water, which create a thin film wrapped around air. Each bubble has a little rainbow of colors in its fragile shell. When light reaches the surface of a bubble, some passes through and some reflects back from the surface to our eyes. The color that gets reflected changes, depending on how thick the layer is where the light hits it. The water **EVAPORATES**, which alters the thickness, causing the swirl of color.

Bubbles are round because the layers of soap and water shrink down in order to take the least amount of space. A **SPHERE** has the smallest surface area. So while they might dance around

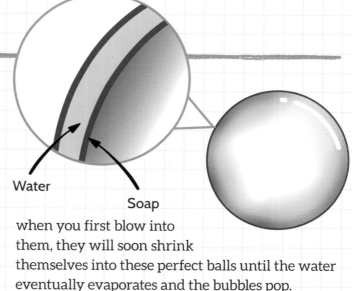

Water

Soap

when you first blow into them, they will soon shrink themselves into these perfect balls until the water eventually evaporates and the bubbles pop.

Glycerin makes them extra strong by reducing the **SURFACE TENSION**. This is the force holding the water **MOLECULES** together at the surface. If surface tension is too strong, the water molecules are pulled together and the bubble pops. Adding glycerin makes the bubbles last longer.

Pizza-box Oven

This is a simple way to make your own oven out of an old pizza box. Pack this project with you the next time you go camping to create the perfect S'mores.

YOU WILL NEED

☑ Empty pizza box
☑ Craft knife
☑ Aluminum foil
☑ Black paper
☑ Clear plastic wrap
☑ Glue stick
☑ Pencil or pen
☑ 2 sticks

FOR THE S'MORES YOU WILL NEED:

☑ Marshmallows
☑ Graham crackers
☑ Chocolate

REHEATING INSTRUCTIONS

1 Measure and mark a 1in (2.5cm) border on the lid of the box. Ask an adult to cut along the sides and bottom of the border and to score along the top line of the border. Bend the cardboard back to create a large doorlike flap.

2 Line the inside of the box (including the side and underside of the lid and the flap) with foil, and glue in place. The reflectiveness of the foil will help heat up the inside of the oven when the sun is shining on it.

3 Line the bottom of the pizza box with black paper, placing it over the foil. The foil is there to reflect the heat and warm up the oven. You don't need to glue in place.

4 Cut a piece of plastic wrap larger than the square cut out of the lid. Stretch it so there are no creases and tape down along all the sides inside the lid. This will help trap the heat from the sun in the oven.

5 To make the S'mores, break the chocolate into chunks and cut the marshmallows into small pieces. Make a graham cracker sandwich with marshmallows and chocolate layered inside.

6 Place the S'mores into the solar oven and close the lid, leaving the flap open. Use two pieces of dowel or sticks to prop open the flap on the lid of the box. Take your oven into the sunshine. Position the oven so the foil-covered lid is facing the sun. The light needs to reflect off the lid and into the box. Check on your S'mores every ten minutes until the chocolate and marshmallows begin to melt.

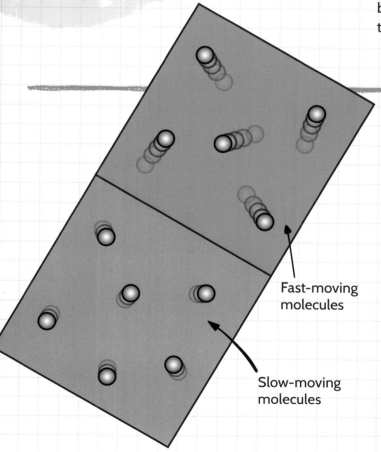

Fast-moving molecules

Slow-moving molecules

SCIENCE MADE SIMPLE

THERMAL ENERGY from the sun enters the box, which heats up the air inside it. The foil reflects heat energy (in the same way that it reflects light) and reduces the amount of energy that can escape from the box, making it warmer than the air outside. Thermal energy is otherwise known as heat energy and is produced when there is a rise in temperature that causes **ATOMS** and **MOLECULES** to move faster and heat up. This energy melts the chocolate and marshmallow and cooks the S'mores!

Cloud Magnets

Make these cool fridge magnets to help you identify and record the different clouds you see each day.

YOU WILL NEED

- ☑ Letter-size (A4) magnetic sheet
- ☑ Blue, gray, and white card
- ☑ Yellow and black markers
- ☑ Toilet/tissue paper
- ☑ PVA glue
- ☑ Gray paint
- ☑ Chopsticks or skewers

Tip

Find out about the different types of clouds. There are four main types: Cirrus, Cumulus, Stratus, and Nimbus.

1 To make the cloud magnets, cut 4 small rectangles from the magnetic sheet. Glue blue card onto 2 sheets, and gray card onto 2 sheets. The blue is for the cumulus and cirrus clouds, and the gray for stratus and nimbus clouds. Cut to size around the magnets, and leave to dry.

2 Draw around a magnet onto white card. Draw a square toward the top of the white card to resemble a polaroid photo, cut out, and glue onto the magnets.

3 To make the clouds, tear up some toilet paper into little pieces. Place in a bowl and cover with water. Leave for about ten minutes to soften. Squeeze out the water from the toilet paper with your hands. Mix with about a tablespoon of PVA glue using a stick.

4 Have a look at pictures of each type of cloud so that you are familiar with what they look like. To make cumulus clouds, use chopsticks (or skewers) to gently place the toilet paper onto the poloroid, making it fluffy. To make cirrus clouds, add small amounts of paper in little whisps to the other blue card. For the stratus clouds, mix some gray paint into the mixture, then add a thin layer all over a gray polaroid. For the cumulonimbus cloud, add some black to the mix to make the cloud a little darker, then make another fluffy cumulus shape.

5 Leave the magnets to dry overnight. You can add a little yellow sun to one of the blue ones or some rain to the nimbus clouds. Label them so you can remember the name for each type of cloud. You can pop them on your fridge or somewhere you will be able to see them every day. Over the next week or two keep a log of the clouds you see, the times you see them, and what the weather was like at that time. What links can you see with the clouds and the weather? Can you see how important the clouds are in determining whether it will be a nice day or a rainy one?

SCIENCE MADE SIMPLE

Clouds are made up of tiny water droplets or **ICE CRYSTALS** floating in the sky. They are created from **WATER VAPOR** that has risen from oceans and rivers.

Clouds play an essential role in creating our weather. When we have fluffy cumulus clouds, the weather is usually pleasant, although it can be windy. These clouds are usually white because they reflect the light from the sun. But if they gather too much moisture they can darken and turn into cumulonimbus. These are heavy, gray clouds that can bring rain and thunder.

Cirrus clouds indicate a change in the weather and often show that fair weather is on its way. They are composed of ice crystals high in the sky and are formed when the air is cold and dry.

Stratus clouds are low in the sky, and create a flat layer that can block out the sun, making the weather colder.

Hot and Cool Colors

If you want to know how to stay cool on a hot, sunny day, this is the activity for you. Have you noticed that when you go out in the sun wearing dark colors you feel hotter than if you wear white? This experiment demonstrates how color affects the temperature of objects.

YOU WILL NEED

- ☑ Bottles or containers (one for each colored piece of paper)
- ☑ Cool water
- ☑ Pitcher
- ☑ Colored paper (including white and black)
- ☑ Sticky tape
- ☑ Thermometer

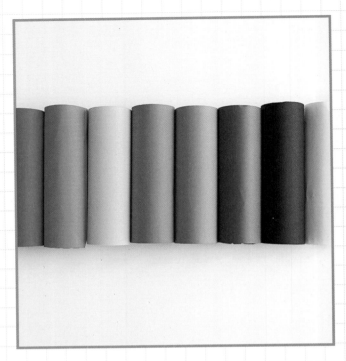

1 Cover a bottle in a colored piece of paper and seal with tape.

2 Repeat to cover each bottle with a different colored piece of paper.

3 Fill a pitcher with water, then use a thermometer to take the temperature, and make a note of it. Pour the water into the bottles.

Take the bottles outside and place in bright sunlight. Leave them to sit for 20 minutes.

4 Measure the temperature of the water in each bottle and note down changes. Repeat this every 20 minutes for an hour. You should see that the water in bottles covered in darker paper is warmer than the lighter colors. The water in the white paper should remain the coolest. In our tests the water in the white bottle only increased by 7.2°F (4°C), compared to the black bottle which increased by 21.6°F (12°C). The lighter colored bottles (pink, yellow, purple) went up by 9–10.8°F (5–6°C) compared to the darker colors (blue, red, green), which increased between 10.8–12.6°F (6–7°C).

SCIENCE MADE SIMPLE

Why does the water in the white bottle stay cooler than the rest? This is because lighter colors are more **REFLECTIVE** than darker colors: White reflects light waves and bounces them back into the air. It absorbs less heat from the sun, keeping the water cooler. Black does the opposite and absorbs **WAVELENGTHS** of light. This means the color takes on the heat, so the temperature is raised. The varying results in the other colors depend on how much **PIGMENT** the color has. You can see this in everyday life. Cars in hot countries are usually light colored so they stay cooler, sunshades are light colored, and you can stay cooler in white clothes during the summer months.

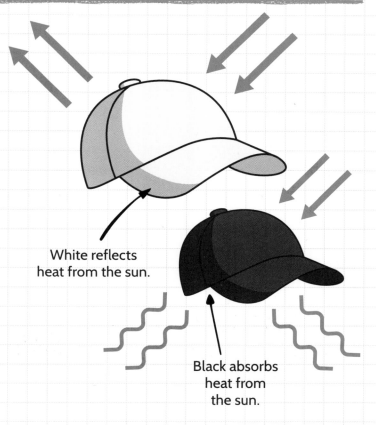

White reflects heat from the sun.

Black absorbs heat from the sun.

Compost in a Bottle

Make a mini-compost collection and discover how organic waste is broken down by microorganisms and turned into nutritious plant food. You can do this experiment quickly and observe it for weeks afterward!

YOU WILL NEED

- ☑ Organic matter
- ☑ Large plastic bottle
- ☑ Sticky tape
- ☑ Water
- ☑ Permanent marker

Tip

Tea is compostable but some tea bags are not, so check before you add to your organic matter collection.

1 Gather together the materials to make the compost. You can include fruit and vegetable scraps, egg shells, compostable tea bags, soil, shredded paper and card, leaves, and grass.

2 Cut off the top quarter of the bottle and set it aside. Don't discard the lid.

3 Add a thin layer of soil to the bottom of the bottle, then a layer of food waste. Add another layer of soil, then some shredded paper. Then layer the items with the soil to the top.

4 With adult help, cut a slit in the cut edge of the top of the bottle so that you can slot it into the top of the compost bottle. Tape it tightly to seal.

5 Open up the lid and pour in about a cup of water. There should be enough water so that it seeps all the way to the bottom. Add a mark at the top to show where the top of the compost comes to. Put the compost in a sunny spot, either outside or on a windowsill if it's not warm enough. Leave it there for a week before checking it.

6 After a week, you should see that your compost has shrunk. This is because it is decomposing (being eaten away by tiny organisms to make smaller parts). If you touch the bottle, you might find that it is warm. This is because the activity of the organisms breaking down the waste produces heat. Check your compost every week. After a month the level of the compost will have shrunk further. What things can you still see in the compost? Some things, like grass and peelings, decompose quickly while others, like eggshells, take much longer. Once your organic materials have decomposed, you can use your compost.

SCIENCE MADE SIMPLE

Composting is a really great way to reduce food waste as well as improving the quality of our soils, which is super important. The organic waste that you put in the bottle became food for tiny little creatures living in the soil. These creatures are called **MICROORGANISMS**, like bacteria, algae, and **FUNGI**. These are so small you can't see them without a microscope. The microorganisms eat the waste and break it into much smaller parts. As the waste **DECOMPOSES**, it sinks down in the bottle. This creates compost—a **NUTRIENT**-rich matter that is great food for plants and essential for healthy soil.

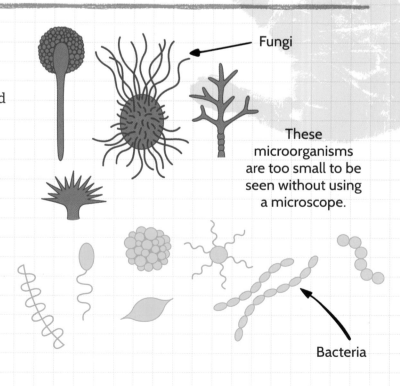

Fungi

These microorganisms are too small to be seen without using a microscope.

Bacteria

Rainbow Kite

Make and fly this colorful kite and learn all about air pressure at the same time.

YOU WILL NEED

- ☑ Tissue paper in a range of colors
- ☑ Sticky back plastic
- ☑ Ball of string
- ☑ 8 pieces of thin dowel
- ☑ Glue gun

1 Draw a diamond shape onto the back of the sticky back plastic. This one is 18in (45cm) high and 17in (43cm) wide. Rip some tissue paper into roughly 1in (2.5cm) squares. Starting at the top of your paper peel back some of the backing and stick the tissue paper down. Work all the way down the diamond, peeling off the backing as you go.

2 Cut a second piece of sticky back plastic paper into a diamond shape making it ½in (1cm) bigger than in Step 1. Peel off the backing and stick on top of the tissue paper. Fold the excess contact paper over to seal the two pieces together.

3 To create the crossbars on the back of the kite, glue two pieces of dowel down the middle next to each other from the top point of the diamond to the bottom. Repeat with more dowel across the kite from the other two corners.

4 Tie a piece of string from the top piece of dowel to the bottom piece making sure there's a little bit of slack in the string. Repeat with another piece of string widthways across the kite from corner to corner. This part is called the bridle.

5 To make the ribbon tail, cut a 20in (0.5 meter) piece of string and tie it onto the bottom of the kite. To make the bows, cut 2½ x 1in (6 x 2.5cm) rectangles of tissue paper. Scrunch each piece of tissue paper in the middle and tie onto your tail string, spacing them out equally.

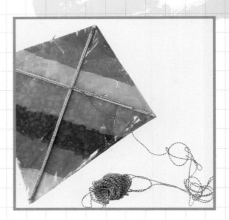

6 Cut a long piece of string, about 13ft (4 meters) and tie onto the string where your two bits of string on the kite meet. Then wrap the other end of the string around a stick. This is called the kite run.

7 Head to a local park, field, or a big open space. Ideally you need a clear day with a moderate breeze. Start by facing away from the wind and hold your kite by the bridle. Let out the string on the stick and when the kite catches the wind let go of the bridle. Once the kite is in the air keep the line taut. Pull on the line to keep the kite up. To land your kite safely simply reel in the kite string.

SCIENCE MADE SIMPLE

When a kite is in the air it has different **FORCES** acting on it. Wind blows all around the kite. Some of that wind hits the kite itself, some goes over it and some under it. Kites have a special shape to help them fly. They are angled so the air moving over the top of the kite moves faster than the air moving under the bottom of the kite. This causes the **AIR PRESSURE** under the kite to be greater than the pressure above it.

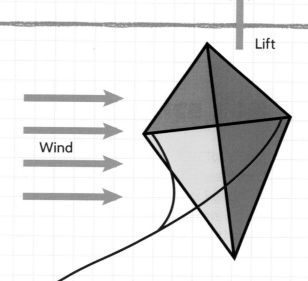

This difference in air pressure causes an upward force called **LIFT**. To launch a kite the lift must be larger than the downward force caused by the weight of the kite. The wind underneath the kite is the one that keeps the kite in the air.

Homemade Slushies

Make your own slushies with a few ingredients and a dash of science. The slushies are best made with fruit juices. You can learn all about freezing points of liquid and the special power of salt in the experiment. For best results, make on a sunny day and serve immediately!

YOU WILL NEED

- ☑ Fruit juice
- ☑ Jar with a lid
- ☑ Ziplock bag (smaller than your jar)
- ☑ Ice cubes
- ☑ Salt
- ☑ Tape
- ☑ Gloves/towel (optional)

1 Put 6-8 ice cubes in a ziplock bag.

2 Add a tablespoon of salt to the ice. Crush the ice a little, press out the air from the bag, and seal tightly. You can tape the bag shut as an extra precaution (to avoid ending up with a salty slushy).

3 Add juice to your jar so it's one-third full. Place the ziplock bag inside the jar and put the lid on the jar. Make sure it's on tightly.

4 Put on your favorite song, crank up the volume, and get shaking! The jar will get cold so you might want to wear gloves or place the jar in a tea towel if it gets too cold! You'll notice the more you shake, foam will form on top of the fruit juice. The juice will start to get colder and ice will start to form in the liquid. If the liquid isn't getting icy you can remove the ziplock bag and add another teaspoon of salt to the bag before resealing.

5 When you've got your desired amount of ice (or your arms are too tired from shaking!), open the jar and discharge the ziplock bag. Pour your drink into a cup and serve with a straw, a cocktail umbrella, and a slice of fruit!

SCIENCE MADE SIMPLE

Salt melts the ice cubes at a faster rate than normal. This is because salt lowers the **FREEZING POINT** of water. As the ice melts it takes heat from the surrounding **LIQUID**, in this case the fruit juice. The melting ice in the bag pulls the heat from the juice and causes **ICE CRYSTALS** to form in the slushie. Shaking the jar helps the juice to freeze more evenly.

Ant Farm Fun

There are trillions of ants on the planet and they are found almost everywhere on Earth, apart from the very coldest climates. Make your own ant farm so you can observe these amazing creatures for a couple of weeks and then return them to their home undisturbed.

YOU WILL NEED

- ☑ 1 large and 1 small jar (to fit inside the big jar)
- ☑ Putty
- ☑ 1 cup of sand
- ☑ 2 cups of soil
- ☑ Small plastic container
- ☑ Compass/sharp knife/ awl
- ☑ Trowel
- ☑ Old sponge
- ☑ Small bit of fruit
- ☑ 2 letter-size (A4) sheets of black card
- ☑ Sticky tape

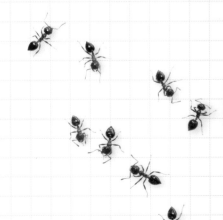

1 Big jars (around 2 pints/1 liter capacity or more) work best for this project. The smaller jar should fit inside the larger one with about 1in (2.5cm) or less of space between. Put the smaller jar into the larger jar. Use a bit of putty on the bottom to keep it in the center.

2 Mix about two cups of soil with 1 cup of sand. Mix in about a tablespoon or two of water if the soil is dry (it should be slightly moist but not wet). Add the soil mixture but do not press it down—the soil should be loose. Stop when you get to about 3in (7.5cm) from the top.

3 Put the lid on the jar and ask an adult to poke some air holes into the top using a compass or awl. Make sure the holes aren't too big as the ants might escape.

4 To provide the ants with food and water, cut off a small chunk from an old sponge and soak it in water. Cut a small chunk of apple (or other fruit) and put them both on top of the soil.

5 Take a plastic pot with a lid to collect your ants (you don't need air holes as you won't be storing the ants there for long). Look for black not red ants (these bite). Lift up plant pots and large rocks and, if you see lots of ants scurrying, there is probably a nest nearby. Dig carefully into the soil to see if you can find them. Use a spoon to carefully scoop ants into your container—you'll need at least 20 or 30. You'll get some soil too but that's okay as you left space in your jar. Only collect ants from one nest or they will kill each other.

6 Tip the ants into the prepared jar and quickly add the lid. Ants prefer to tunnel in the dark, so make a tube for the jar with sheets of black card and tape. Leave the ants in a cool place with the card tube in place for a day or two.

7 Now your ant farm is finished, you can check back on them regularly and see how they progress over a couple of weeks. You should see the ants start to create tunnels and scurry about. Observe the way they greet each other as they pass. Try picking one ant and following its journey around the jar. You may notice that when two ants meet they greet each other by touching antennae (the feelers on their head that can detect scents). This is a way to recognize each other as part of the same colony and communicate useful information. After a couple of weeks you can take the jar back to the ant nest and open the lid to allow the ants to return to their home.

SCIENCE MADE SIMPLE

Ants really are impressive insects. They can adapt to live in almost any **HABITAT** in the world in complex, highly organized social colonies, or family groups. Each ant has a specific role—be it forager, builder, nurse (all of which are worker ants), or drone, which is the male reproductive ant.

They are also fantastic communicators and interact using pheromones, a type of scent emitted to send specific signals. They recognize one another this way and can spot an intruder instantly. If an ant from a different colony enters the nest the ants release pheromones to signal to the colony that they are potentially under attack.

They are also impressive builders. They can build huge chambers, ventilation shafts, bridges, and tunnels. The tunnels they build connect the different chambers of the nest. Living underground provides them with protection from predators and the weather and allows them to expand their home.

And they are also super strong. Some ants can lift objects up to 100 times their body weight. This is the equivalent of you being able to lift and lug around a truck!

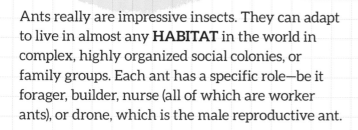

Mini Fire Extinguisher

How do you put out a match without blowing on it? Try this experiment and you will discover how and why.

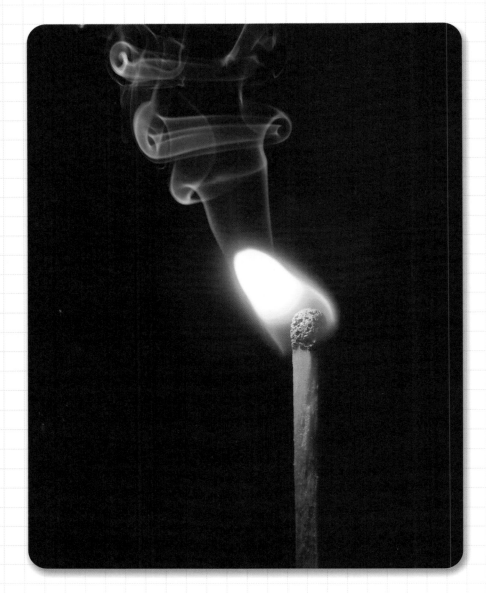

YOU WILL NEED

- ☑ Cup
- ☑ Vinegar
- ☑ Bicarbonate of soda
- ☑ Match

SAFETY FIRST!

This activity needs adult supervision.

1 Pour a small amount of vinegar into a cup so the cup is roughly 1in (2.5cm) full.

2 Add 1 teaspoon of bicarbonate of soda to the cup. It will bubble up and foam. The vinegar and bicarbonate of soda react, creating the gas carbon dioxide (CO_2).

3 Quickly light a match and hover it over the cup.

4 The match should extinguish very quickly!

SCIENCE MADE SIMPLE

This works because the **CHEMICAL REACTION** of the vinegar and bicarbonate of soda replaced the **OXYGEN (O_2)** the fire needs in order to burn with **CARBON DIOXIDE (CO_2)**. This causes the match to go out. This is how real fire extinguishers often work, on a much larger scale. They spray foam that cools the flames and removes the oxygen from the fire.

DIY Wind Vane

Wind vanes are used to measure the direction of the wind. The word "vane" comes from an old English word for "flag". Originally wind vanes were fabric banners attached to medieval towers. Knowing which direction the wind is coming from is still important today, especially for people whose work depends on the weather like farmers and sailors.

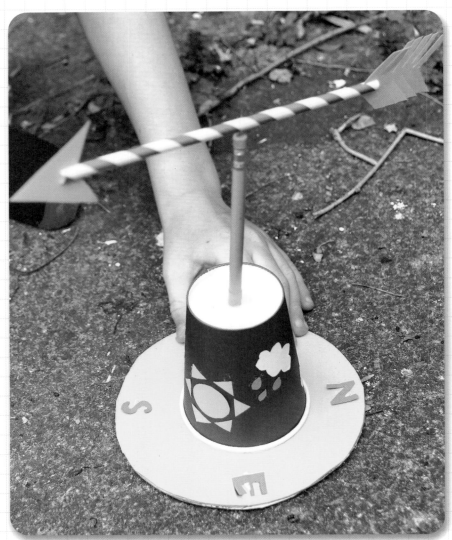

YOU WILL NEED
- ☑ Cardboard
- ☑ Colored card
- ☑ Glue stick
- ☑ Strong glue
- ☑ Paper cup
- ☑ Paper straw
- ☑ Sewing pin
- ☑ Pencil with eraser
- ☑ Compass

1 Draw around a bowl onto cardboard (approximately 6in/15cm) and cut out a circle of cardboard. Draw around the circle onto colored card, cut it out, and stick it onto the cardboard.

2 Decorate the paper cup with scraps of colored card. You could do a weather theme or choose any design you like.

3 Measure and mark the centerpoint in the base of the paper cup and push the pencil through the hole. Secure in place using strong glue.

4 Glue the paper cup to the center of the circle.

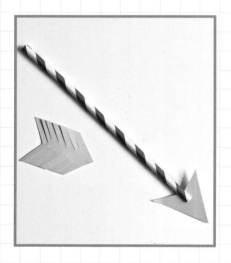

5 Cut a triangle out of colored card. Cut a feather shape for the tail–this should be about ½in (1cm) wider than the arrowhead. This allows the end to catch the wind. Cut two slits about ½in (1cm) long at both ends of the straw. Slot the arrowhead and feathers into the straw. Add glue to hold in place.

6 Carefully push the sewing pin through the middle of the straw and into the eraser on the pencil. Make sure the arrow can spin around. On the base add the letters N, S, E, W for compass points North, South, East, and West.

7 Head outside and use a compass to identify North. Hold the wind vane around the base and position yourself so the North on the vane matches the North on the compass. When the wind blows the arrow should spin and point in the direction the wind is coming from. See the science explanation below to understand why this happens.

SCIENCE MADE SIMPLE

The wind vane works from the **FORCE** of the wind spinning the arrow around. The arrow points in the direction the wind is coming from. This is because the tail of the arrow is wider than the arrowhead: When the wind blows it exerts more force on the tail because it has a larger surface area compared to the arrowhead. This causes the tail to swing away from the wind leaving the arrowhead to point in the direction the wind is coming from.

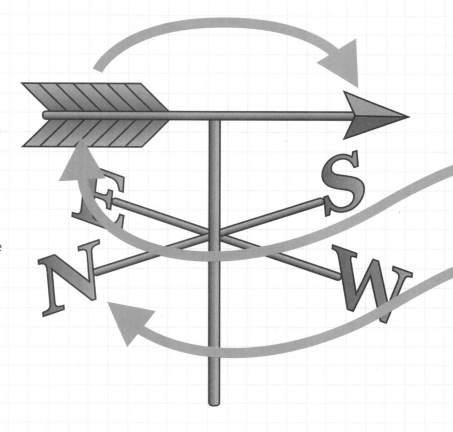

Mud Bombs

This is a fantastically messy experiment that's great outside for minimal clean up. Wear old clothes and make sure you stand a little way back otherwise you'll get totally splatted with mud!

YOU WILL NEED
- ☑ Mud
- ☑ Water
- ☑ 2 Alka-Seltzer tablets
- ☑ Small plastic container with loose fitting lid
- ☑ Bowl

1 Grab a container and head outside on a soil hunt. Collect enough soil so your container is one-third full. Look for soil that is smooth and not full of pebbles!

2 Tip the soil into a larger bowl and add water to it to create a mud pie that's the consistency of thick cream. Fill the small container about two-thirds full with the mud mixture.

3 Take it outside where there is space for you to stand back (and not get covered in mud!). Break up two Alka-Seltzer tablets and put them in the mixture.

4 Quickly put the lid on and turn the container upside down. Take a step back!

5 You should notice that bubbles will start to form in the container. Wait for the explosion. The container should fly up in the air and mud will splat everywhere! You can fill the container up and try it all again. Try experimenting using more Alka-Seltzer tablets or pots of different sizes and shapes to see what gives the biggest explosion.

SCIENCE MADE SIMPLE

You can see that when you add an Alka-Seltzer tablet to a liquid it dissolves. As it does so, it releases a gas called **CARBON DIOXIDE** (CO_2). This forms bubbles inside the muddy mixture. As the container is closed there is nowhere for the CO_2 to escape, which causes pressure to build inside the container. Eventually the pressure gets so much that it causes the lid to pop off and make the container fly up into the air. The CO_2 is then free to escape and mud goes everywhere!

Color-changing Petals

Like a magic trick, you can change the color of petals—and learn about how plants take in water at the same time.

YOU WILL NEED

- ☑ Light-colored flowers
- ☑ Food coloring
- ☑ Water
- ☑ Glass jar

1 Head outside on a flower hunt. Look for flowers with white or light-colored petals, such as daisies. Pick the flowers near the ground so you have long stems. Collect a small bunch and make sure not to pick too many—especially if there are only a few in the first place.

2 Fill a jar with water and add food coloring to the water. Give it a stir to mix. Snip the very end off each stem and put the flowers into the jar and leave overnight.

3 Take the flowers out of the jar, dab the end of the stems dry, and examine what has happened to the petals. Have they changed color? You should see that the petals have taken on the color of the water!

4 You can try different food colorings to see which give the most vibrant colored petals. You could even try carefully splitting the stem in half and putting each half in different colored water for a two-tone flower!

Exploding Petal Potion

Head outside to the garden or your local park and look for petals, small flowers, grass, leaves, and a small stick (for stirring). Put your nature finds into a jar or cup and half fill the cup with water. Add a few drops of food coloring to the potion and stir with your stick. Add a tablespoon of bicarbonate of soda and stir to combine. Now for the magic! Pour vinegar into the mixture and take a step back. The mixture will foam up and out of the cup creating a lovely colored foam filled with petals and leaves!

SCIENCE MADE SIMPLE

The petals change color because plants have a system of tubes, called a **XYLEM**, which carry water upward, similar to when you suck up a drink through a straw. The water travels from the roots of a plant, through the stem, and into the plant's leaves and flowers. This scientific process is called **CAPILLARY ACTION**.

Melted Crayon Artwork

Learn all about how the melting of a wax crayon is a "reversible change of state." It's best to do this on a hot sunny day and, preferably, when it's not windy, so your wax crayon shavings don't fly everywhere!

YOU WILL NEED

- ☑ Wax crayons
- ☑ Sharpener
- ☑ Colored paper
- ☑ Sunshine!

1 If there are any wrappers on the crayons remove them. Then use a sharpener to create shavings from the different colored crayons. Put each color into a paint palette or similar to keep them separate ready for your art.

2 Head outside and use the crayon shavings to create a picture by sprinkling them onto a piece of paper. You can arrange them in patterns or create pictures using the different colors.

3 Leave the artwork in the sun for at least an hour, depending on how hot it is, and your crayon shavings should melt onto the page. Check on the artwork after 30 minutes to see how the melting is going. Can you notice if any colors are melting faster than others? You should see that darker colors melt faster than lighter colors. Once the wax has cooled down the colors will blend into each other and create a lovely picture.

SCIENCE MADE SIMPLE

When you leave crayons out in the sun, the crayons heat up and melt, changing from a **SOLID** to a **LIQUID**. When the wax cools down it changes back into a solid again. This is called a **REVERSIBLE CHANGE OF STATE**. The wax crayons look and feel different when melted, but they return to their original state once cooled.

When the crayons are heated up, the ingredients in them separate. The speed at which each crayon melts is down to the pigments in the colors. Darker colors such as black melt faster than lighter colors such as white. This is because black absorbs more light and white reflects the heat. This means that it doesn't take in as much heat and takes longer to melt.

DIY Quicksand

This amazing quicksand can be molded and formed into shapes. But, as soon as hands or objects are still or moving slowly, the quicksand turns into a liquid.

YOU WILL NEED

- ☑ 5 cups cornstarch
- ☑ 5 cups sand
- ☑ Water
- ☑ Large container (such as a washing-up bowl)
- ☑ Small plastic toys

1 Combine the cornstarch and sand in a large container. We used 5 cups of each but this would work with any quantity as long as they are equal.

2 Slowly add in water and mix the starch and sand together. The mixture should be moldable but not too wet. Mix as you go until you get the right consistency.

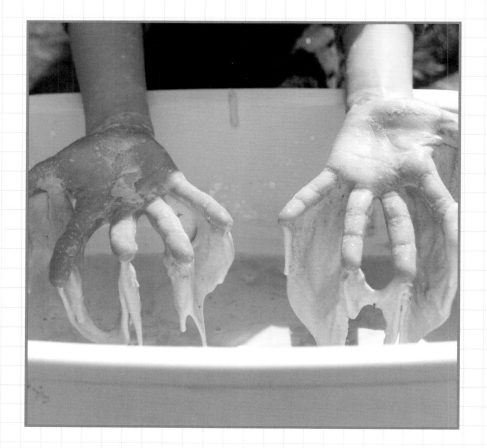

3 Take it outside and add a few toys to the sand. Watch as they sit on the surface of the sand at first, then gradually sink in. If you get your hands in to save them, you'll see that if you squeeze the sand it will feel hard but if you open your hands the sand will run through them like a liquid.

SAND SLIME

This super stretchy sand is fun to play with and to make. You will need PVA glue, sand, and slime activator. Combine equal parts of PVA glue and sand. Add the slime activator little by little and stir until you get a slime consistency.

SCIENCE MADE SIMPLE

The homemade quicksand is a cool **NON-NEWTONIAN FLUID**, which means it acts like a **SOLID** and a **LIQUID**. Its consistency depends on how much pressure you put on it. This is because the **PARTICLES** in the cornstarch are actually a solid, suspended in the water. When you apply pressure, they stick together, and make the substance behave like a solid. When you let the substance drip though your hands, it behaves like a liquid because the particles in the cornstarch are able to separate and slip around your hands.

Slime is another cool example of a non-Newtonian fluid, meaning it is neither a liquid nor a solid and has properties of both. Slime doesn't have its own shape and will fill any container it is put in. Slime is made up of polymers, which are long chains of **MOLECULES** that bind together when the ingredients are mixed. Chemical bonds are formed when the PVA glue and slime activator are mixed. Slime activators join layers of polymers together in a process called **CROSS-LINKING**.

Shadow Art

Make pictures that create shadows on the ground and use shadows to draw your own art! You'll need a nice sunny day for these projects, so remember your sunscreen when you head outside.

YOU WILL NEED

- ☑ Colored paper
- ☑ Sticky back plastic
- ☑ Leaves, petals, grass
- ☑ Tissue paper
- ☑ Glue stick

1 Find leaves, petals, and grass for your picture (the materials you find need to lie flat). Cut a piece of sticky back plastic a little bigger than the size you want your picture to be. Peel the backing away and place it sticky side up on a table. Arrange the flowers and leaves into a picture. The picture should be something that is easily recognizable as a silhouette, so keep your design simple.

2 Cut another piece of sticky back plastic the same size as before. Peel off the back and stick on top of your picture. Trim the edges so there are no sticky parts. Cut a frame out of colored paper and glue your picture onto the back of the frame. Position your art with the sun shining through it and near the ground. You'll see your picture in silhouette on the ground, without any color.

3 You can also use other materials to create a picture and then compare which makes the best shadow art. Try using shapes cut out from colored paper or tissue paper.

4 Position your tissue-paper art with the sun shining through it and near the ground. You'll see your picture in silhouette on the ground with a hint of color! The tissue paper is translucent so it allows some light through. That is why you see the outline of the picture and some of the color detail in the shadow.

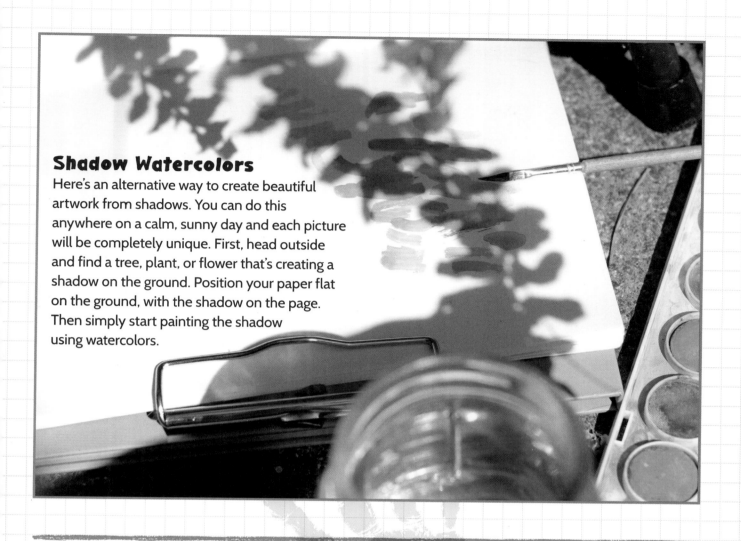

Shadow Watercolors

Here's an alternative way to create beautiful artwork from shadows. You can do this anywhere on a calm, sunny day and each picture will be completely unique. First, head outside and find a tree, plant, or flower that's creating a shadow on the ground. Position your paper flat on the ground, with the shadow on the page. Then simply start painting the shadow using watercolors.

SCIENCE MADE SIMPLE

A shadow is a dark shape made by something that blocks light from a light source. You will probably have noticed that when the sun is in front of you, the outline of your body is on the ground behind you. This is because you are blocking the light from the sun to the ground, which creates a shadow. For a shadow to form, the object must be **OPAQUE** (meaning you can't see through it) or **TRANSLUCENT** (it allows some light to pass through). The colored paper and leaves used in the shadow art are both opaque so that's why you clearly see the picture as a shadow without any color. The sticky back plastic used is transparent and doesn't create any shadows because light can pass straight through it.

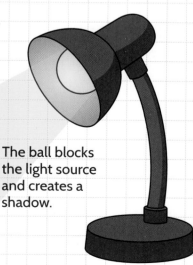

The ball blocks the light source and creates a shadow.

Stick Slingshot

Learn about the forces of kinetic and potential energy with this cool stick slingshot.

YOU WILL NEED

- ☑ Y-shaped piece of wood
- ☑ Pruning shears
- ☑ About 24in (60cm) elastic cord
- ☑ Scrap of fabric
- ☑ Scrap of fusible interface
- ☑ Eyelets
- ☑ Hammer
- ☑ Ribbon
- ☑ Embroidery thread or twine for decoration (optional)
- ☑ Craft glue

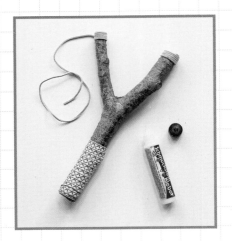

1 Head out to find the perfect stick for your slingshot. You need to find one with an even joint creating a Y shape. Find wood that is not dead and brittle and about ¾in (2cm) in diameter. Ask an adult to help cut the wood to the right shape and trim off any excess twigs or rough bits. If you like you can remove the bark.

2 Add a line of glue down the back of the handle, about 4in (10cm) long, and wrap ribbon around it to give you a smooth surface to grip. If you like you can add some decorative embroidery thread or ribbon to the stick too. Here we are adding some suede twine to the top of the slingshot.

3 With adult supervision, use an iron to press and glue a scrap of fusible interfacing onto a piece of fabric. Cut down to a rectangle measuring about 3 x 2in (7 x 5cm).

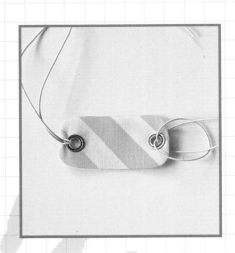

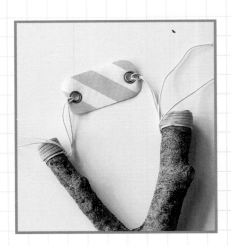

4 Add the eyelets and hammer into place, following the manufacturer's guidelines. Cut to round the edges of the fabric if you like.

5 Cut two 12in (30cm) lengths of elastic. Fold each one in half and feed the folded end through the eyelet. Pull the ends of the elastic through the loop to create a knot.

6 Tie the other ends loosely to the top of each side of the slingshot. The length depends on the size of your stick, but don't tie it so that it is taut. Test it out by pulling back the fabric and adjust to your preferred length.

7 Once you are happy tie tightly, trim the excess, and add a dot of glue to the knot to stop it unraveling. Now load up your slingshot! Do NOT aim at anyone or put anything too hard in it—rocks and marbles are a bad idea. But try acorns, little pinecones, and seed pods. Hold the slingshot firmly in one hand and use your other hand to pinch your ammo in the fabric and pull back the elastic. Aim and fire! How far can you get? Mark your starting point and furthest points in chalk to record the distances.

SCIENCE MADE SIMPLE

When you pull the elastic of the slingshot back the elastic stretches, transferring the energy from you to stored **POTENTIAL ENERGY** in the elastic. The more you stretch it, the more potential energy the elastic has. When you release the elastic, it quickly springs back to its un-stretched form, transferring the energy to the ammo and propelling it forward. This is called **KINETIC ENERGY**, the energy of movement.

Slingshots and catapults have been around for thousands of years. In ancient times, people used vines and animal skins as slingshots to hunt animals.

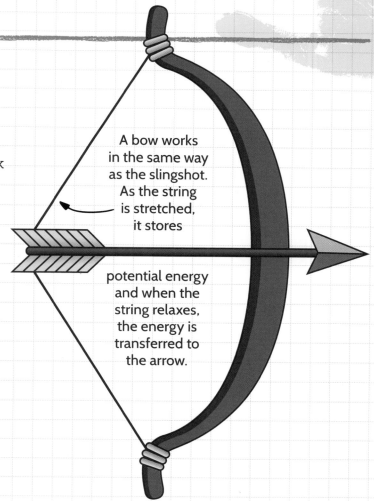

A bow works in the same way as the slingshot. As the string is stretched, it stores potential energy and when the string relaxes, the energy is transferred to the arrow.

Solar Still

This is a really cool survival tool that uses heat from the sun to purify water, which can provide people with safe water and save lives. The good thing is that it is super easy to make. You do need a warm sunny day to do this project, and it is best to start in the morning as the still takes time to work.

YOU WILL NEED
- ☑ A large bowl
- ☑ A small dish (to fit inside the bowl)
- ☑ Half a cup of salt
- ☑ Water
- ☑ Plastic wrap
- ☑ Heavy rock

SAFETY FIRST!
Try this with tap water or rainwater. Do not attempt to use water from the sea.

1 Place the small dish inside the large bowl and fill the large bowl with water, making sure it doesn't go above the height of the dish.

2 Remove the dish and mix in about half a cup of salt. Give it a good stir until it is dissolved. Now dip your finger in the water and taste it. It should taste salty and horrible!

3 Replace the dish into the middle of the bowl and cover with plastic wrap.

4 Take the bowl outside and place it in a spot that will be in full sun for as much of the day as possible. Find a nice big rock and place it on the center. Push it down a little if you need to so that the rock creates a dip in the center of the plastic wrap.

5 Check the still after a couple of hours. You should see that the warmth of the sun has heated up the water and made it evaporate, forming small droplets of water in the form of condensation on the plastic wrap.

6 If you gently lift up the rock, you might see a droplet on the plastic wrap underneath where the rock was. The condensation builds up and trickles down to the bottom, dripping into the dish. This is how you collect water.

7

After several hours, remove the rock and plastic wrap and observe how much water you collected. It probably won't be a lot! But it will be fresh, drinkable water. Taste it to check!

SCIENCE MADE SIMPLE

The heat of the sun warms the water in the bowl and causes it to **EVAPORATE**, meaning it changes from a **LIQUID** to a **GAS (WATER VAPOR)**. In doing so it leaves behind all the impurities or salt in the water below. This vapor then hits the plastic wrap, which cools it down, turning it back to droplets of liquid—a reversal of evaporation called **CONDENSATION**. The droplets run down the plastic wrap where they drip into the dish.

The solar still works in a similar way to the Earth's **WATER CYCLE**, the continuous movement of water on Earth. Water from the seas, lakes, and rivers evaporates and rises to form clouds where it cools and returns to the Earth as rain and snow.

Obviously if you were stranded on a desert island you wouldn't have a bowl or plastic wrap. What could you use instead? What about digging a hole instead of using a bowl, and using a large shell or even a bit of coconut for the small dish. Thanks to the blight of plastic on our planet you'd probably be able to find an old plastic bag to use for the plastic wrap. You'd also need to make it a lot bigger than in this experiment to collect enough water to survive.

Star Sewing Cards

Our night skies are mapped out into groups of stars called constellations. These form pictures, a bit like a giant dot-to-dot puzzle. You can turn them into sewing cards to keep! First of all, do a spot of star gazing.

FOR STAR GAZING, YOU WILL NEED

- ☑ Blanket/reclining deck chair
- ☑ Binoculars (optional)
- ☑ Star wheel or map
- ☑ Flashlight
- ☑ Sketchpad and pencil
- ☑ Warm drink (optional!)

On a clear night, gather together the equipment and head outside. Lie back and stare up at the sky. Give your eyes a minute to adjust to the darkness and then see what you can identify. Use a star wheel if you have one, or a map to help. Can you see the moon? What constellations can you see? They are hard to find at first, but after you've found them once they will be much easier to spot. Keep a note of which constellations you saw and sketch them out if you like to remember them. This way you can make them into the sewing cards.

FOR THE CARDS, YOU WILL NEED

- ☑ Sheet of half letter (A5) thick card
- ☑ Selection of paints, including navy blue
- ☑ Stiff paintbrush
- ☑ Hole punch
- ☑ Large needle
- ☑ White yarn or embroidery thread

1 Start by painting a sheet of half letter (A5) card navy blue for the night sky.

2 Now head outside for the messy bit. Dip a stiff paintbrush into galaxy colored paints—pink, blue, purple, and white—and flick them on to the card using your thumb. You should get a lovely starry background for your sewing cards.

3 Leave the card to dry and then cut it into quarters.

4 Mark in pencil the constellations you observed onto each one. You can also look at pictures of constellations online.

5 Use a large needle and white yarn to sew between the holes in the card and form the constellations.

SCIENCE MADE SIMPLE

Why not try and find out about the stars you can see outside your bedroom window. Our planet spins on its **AXIS** and moves around the Sun, so the stars you see will vary depending on the time you're looking, the month of the year, and where you are in the world.

To figure out what you're looking at in the sky it can help to use a map. You can download apps on smartphones that allow you to point your phone at the sky and identify stars. Or you can buy or print out a Star Wheel based on where you are in the world. This is a circular map that represents the sky and the stars you can see in it. The edge of the circle is the horizon, and the center is the bit directly above your head. To use it, you rotate the wheel to match the current date and time and it will tell you what you can see.

The Earth rotates around the Sun, which is our nearest star.

Sunscreen Painting

Here's a simple experiment with a really big lesson—the importance of sunscreen. You can do this one next time you're out on a sunny day. If you don't have a paintbrush handy you can use your finger to paint a design. It's best to use construction paper as it's thicker and more durable than regular paper.

YOU WILL NEED
- ☑ Cream sunscreen
- ☑ Small paintbrush
- ☑ Colored construction paper
- ☑ Small dish

1 Squeeze out the sunscreen into a little dish. This will make it easier to paint with.

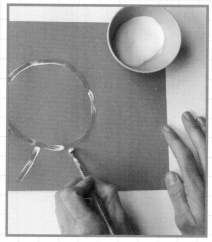

2 Use a paintbrush to paint your design onto the construction paper. You can paint a sun like this one or anything you like. Make sure you leave some of the paper unpainted. Try to only paint a thin layer of sunscreen and don't leave any white marks on the paper.

3 Take your design out into a sunny spot and leave it in the sun. You might need to weigh the corners down with a few pebbles to keep it in place. Don't worry if you have a little bit of white residue from the sun cream on the picture. Leave your artwork out for a few hours.

4 After a while, the paper will bleach and fade in the areas where there is no sunscreen. The superhero chemicals in the sunscreen absorb the harmful UV rays from the sun and stop the paper fading. The sun has the same effect on your skin, except that instead of fading it, it burns and darkens.

SCIENCE MADE SIMPLE

Applying sunscreen can feel icky and it's a pain having to put it on. But it really is important you have it on when you're outside, especially when it's sunny. Without it, the sun burns your skin, causes your skin to age prematurely, and can even cause skin cancer.

The sun emits powerful waves called ultraviolet (UV) radiation. **UVA** and **UVB**, two of the sun's ultraviolet rays, can be harmful to the skin. Sunscreen acts as a protective barrier to those rays. There are two types of suncream—mineral and chemical. Mineral sunscreens contain two minerals, zinc oxide and titanium dioxide. These sit on your skin and act to reflect the sun's rays, like a mirror. They often look white when you put them on. Chemical sunscreens absorb the sun's rays like a sponge. The ingredients absorb the UV radiation, convert the rays into heat and then release that heat from the skin. Sunscreen is very clever!

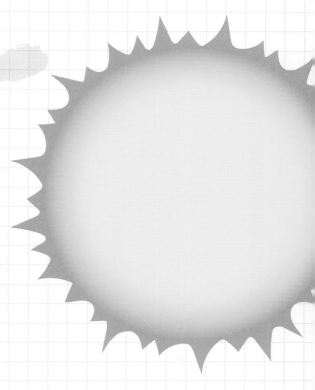

Solar Disco

Here's an easy experiment to do on a sunny day. Raid your recycling for some plastic bottles and a cardboard box and get outside to learn about how light refracts.

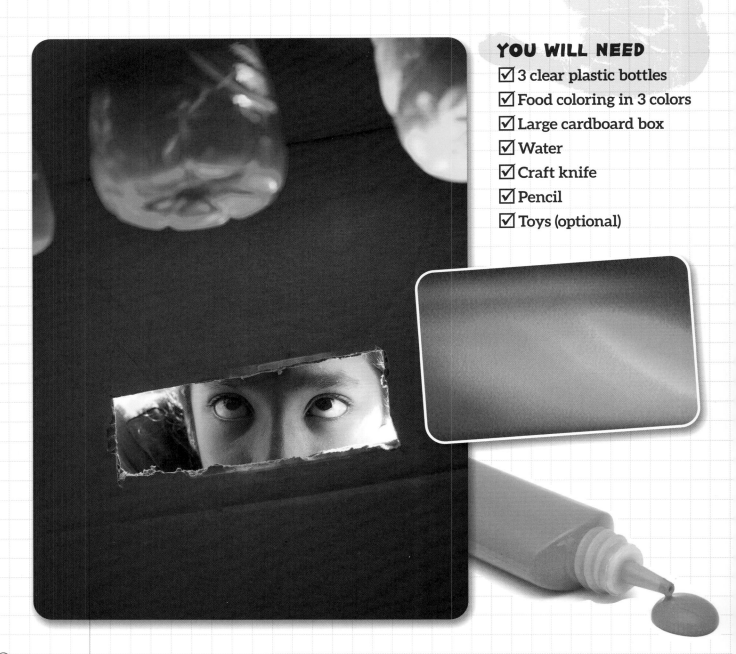

YOU WILL NEED

- ☑ 3 clear plastic bottles
- ☑ Food coloring in 3 colors
- ☑ Large cardboard box
- ☑ Water
- ☑ Craft knife
- ☑ Pencil
- ☑ Toys (optional)

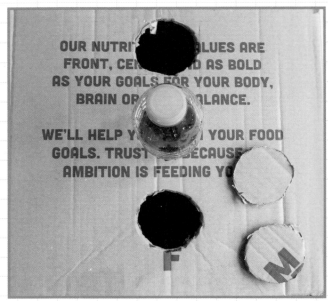

1 Trace around the base of your bottles evenly onto the bottom of a box, spacing out your circles. This will be the top of your solar disco.

2 Cut out the circles making sure they're a little smaller than the ones drawn and check that your bottles fit into the holes. Adjust the size until the bottles fit. The bottles should sit halfway pushed in. Take the bottles out.

3 Fill the bottles up with water mixed with bright food coloring.

4 Position the box so the side with the cut out holes is on top. Then make the peep hole on one of the larger sides of the box. Cut a rectangle one-third of the way down from the top in the center, measuring roughly 2 x 8in (5 x 20cm).

5 Take the disco outside and put the bottles in the top. Then fill your disco with toys, pop some tunes on, and get the party started. Get a friend to twist the bottles while you look through the hole. You'll notice lines of colors in the box that move when the bottles are twisted!

When light meets a water droplet, it is refracted, causing it to disperse into seven colors and form a rainbow.

SCIENCE MADE SIMPLE

So how does your little disco work? It's all to do with **REFRACTION**. When the light hits the colored water in the bottle it slows down and bends in a different direction. This is called light refraction. Since the bottle is round, light is hitting the colored water at different angles. This means that the direction the light bends in will vary, creating pretty patterns on the inside of the box. Wiggling the bottles as the sun hits them causes the light inside the box to move and create a disco effect!

Mandala Coasters

Constructing the mandala is a calming activity and a nice one to do outside. If you want the mandalas to last longer you could try pressing your flowers and leaves before you attach them to the clay (you will need to do this a week or two beforehand).

See page 112 for how to do this.

YOU WILL NEED

☑ Ball of clay (adult-handful sized)

☑ Rolling pin

☑ Circular cookie cutter

☑ Leaves, petals, small flowers

☑ Plastic wrap

☑ Parchment paper

1 Head outside to look for small leaves, flowers, petals, and grass. You need to collect a handful of each as you'll be using them to make a repeating pattern. On a piece of parchment paper, roll out the clay to a thickness of about ½in (1cm). Use a cookie cutter to cut a circle from the clay. You can re-roll your clay to make a few more.

2 Take one of the clay circles and set the others aside in some plastic wrap. Start in the middle of the clay circle and place a small flower in the center of the clay. Push it into the clay so that it stays in place.

3 Build up the repeating pattern, working from the middle outward to the edge of the circle making sure you push the leaves and petals into the clay. Repeat to make more coasters. Leave the clay overnight to harden.

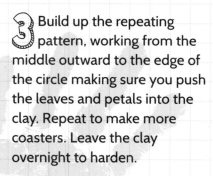

4 If you like you can add a coat of varnish for shine or leave them natural as we have. You could use them as coasters to put your drinks on outside or place them in flower beds as a pretty decoration. Bear in mind that they might get soggy if left out in the rain so bring them inside if it looks like gray skies!

SCIENCE MADE SIMPLE

MANDALAS are **SYMMETRICAL** designs believed to represent different aspects of the universe and are used in meditation in Buddhism and Hinduism. The word mandala means "circle" in Sanskrit and they are believed to have originated from India in the eighth to the twelfth centuries. A mandala is special because it has elements of symmetry, which means it is the same on both sides. You can see symmetry all around you in the world. See if you can spot symmetry in something the next time you head outside. For example, look for symmetry on the wings of a butterfly, or the petals on a flower, or in snowflakes. The design of a mandala is special because it has two types of symmetry (**BILATERAL** and **RADIAL**), which makes it fascinating to look at.

Scrap Vegetables

Did you know you can grow new vegetables from leftover peelings and scraps? What a great way to learn where your veggies come from and how they can regrow from almost nothing!

YOU WILL NEED

- ☑ Vegetable peelings and scraps
- ☑ Knife
- ☑ Compost
- ☑ Plant pots or an area of soil to plant out
- ☑ Shallow bowl
- ☑ Water

Tip

We typically only eat the orange root of a carrot, but did you know you can use the stalks and leaves as well? Try adding them to sauces and salads, or even pesto. If you leave your carrots to grow, they will eventually produce pretty white flowers.

Lettuce

1 Lettuces are really easy to regrow. They won't turn into a full new lettuce, but will give you a few delicious baby leaves. Start by cutting about 1in (2.5cm) off the bottom.

2 Place the bottoms in a small, shallow bowl of water, cut-side up.

3 Put the dish on a sunny window sill. Change the water every couple of days and make sure it doesn't dry out. You should see after a few days that leaves are starting to sprout from the center.

4 After about 10 days you should have some new baby leaves, which you can chop off and eat.

Carrots and Parsnips

1 Cut the stalk ends of the carrots or parsnips, leaving about 1in (2.5cm) of the vegetable intact. If there is some green on the stalk this is better for regrowing, but not essential. Place the carrot tops cut-side down in a container with shallow water. Place the container in a warm sunny spot and top up the water as needed so that the container doesn't dry out.

2 After around a week you should see new shoots coming out the top of the carrots!

3 Once the stalks are fairly sturdy, you can transfer your carrot tops to some pots filled with compost. Cover the root with about 1in (2.5cm) of soil and water after planting. If it's cold, keep the carrots indoors until it warms up outside.

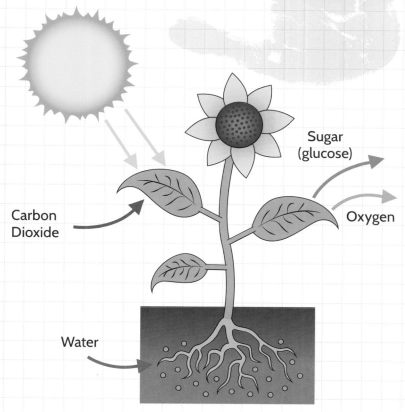

Sugar (glucose)

Oxygen

Carbon Dioxide

Water

PLANTS NEED A FEW THINGS TO GROW:

- Sunlight allows plants to make their own food. They use a process called **PHOTOSYNTHESIS** to take energy from light and store it inside the plant.
- Soil gives the plant essential **NUTRIENTS** like nitrogen, potassium, and phosphorus.
- Water helps the plant carry these nutrients, via its roots, from the soil to the plant.
- Air is needed as plants use **OXYGEN (O_2)** just like we do. They also take **CARBON DIOXIDE (CO_2)** out of the air and use it to make sugar.
- Temperatures need to be stable for plants to thrive. When it is too hot or too cold, the plant will suffer.

Sand Volcano

Learn about chemical reactions while playing with sand! You can do this simple experiment in a sandpit if you have one, or place sand on a tray if not.

YOU WILL NEED

- ☑ Cup of white vinegar
- ☑ Food coloring
- ☑ Pitcher
- ☑ ½ cup baking soda
- ☑ 2–3 buckets of sand
- ☑ Jar or tall cup
- ☑ Tray with sides
- ☑ Pebbles, leaves, twigs, and plastic animals (optional)

Tip

This can get very messy so make sure you do this activity outside!

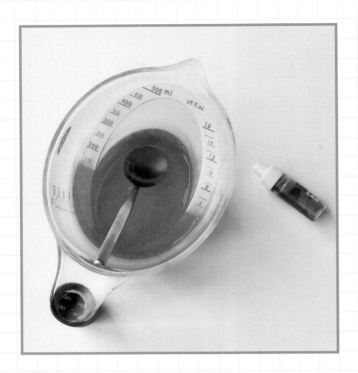

1 In a pitcher, mix a cup of vinegar with food coloring to make your lava base. Place the sand into a tray with sides.

2 Place a jar or tall cup in your sand. Pat the sand around the jar into a volcano shape.

3 You can add things into the sand, such as small twigs for trees, pebbles, or plastic animals.

4 Put the baking soda into the jar.

5 Now for the eruption! When you are ready, pour the vinegar into the jar and watch what happens. When the vinegar hits the baking soda a chemical reaction occurs, causing the liquid to bubble up and foam and erupt from the volcano.

6 After the mixture has settled and soaked into the sand, observe the difference in your volcano now. You should see little craters in the sand. Can you work out what has caused these? They are formed by all the little bubbles that were produced in the chemical reaction.

SCIENCE MADE SIMPLE

The eruption is created in your volcano when you mix together vinegar and baking soda. Vinegar is made of an **ACID** and the baking soda is made of a chemical called a **BASE**. When you mix vinegar and baking soda together they react and produce **CARBON DIOXIDE (CO_2)** (not all acid/base reactions make carbon dioxide). This creates a big frothy eruption of **LIQUID** and **BUBBLES**. You could try this with other containers and see the difference. What happens if you do the same experiment with a plastic bottle? You should see that your eruption is much more explosive as the liquid doesn't have as much space to escape.

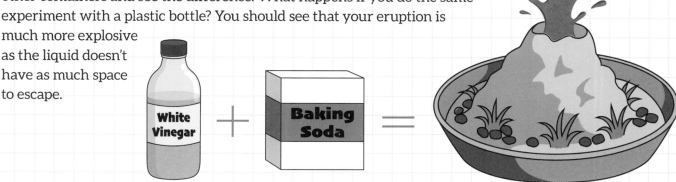

Egg Drop Challenge

Take the challenge and have a cracking good time, while learning all about gravity and different types of energy. Challenge a friend to see who can make the sturdiest casing for your egg to create the least damage. After the count of three drop your eggs from the same height. The egg with the least cracks has the sturdiest protector. Use hard-boiled eggs to reduce the mess when they are dropped.

YOU WILL NEED
- ☑ Hard-boiled eggs
- ☑ Paper
- ☑ Cotton wool
- ☑ Paper-towel tube
- ☑ Newspaper
- ☑ Shredded paper
- ☑ Bubble wrap
- ☑ Rubber band
- ☑ Card
- ☑ Sponge
- ☑ Egg carton
- ☑ Yogurt pots
- ☑ Paper straws
- ☑ Glue gun
- ☑ Tape

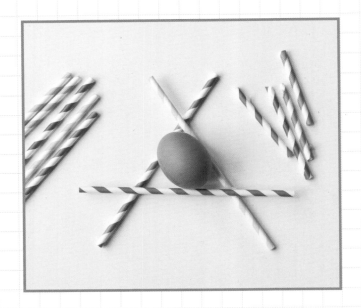

1 Paper straw protector: Glue three straws together in a triangle shape. Make the triangle big enough for your egg to sit in. Place the egg inside.

2 Cut two straws in half and glue around the egg to create a pyramid. Trim off the excess ends of the straws. Once you've tested your egg protector you can try doubling up the straws to see if that makes it even sturdier.

3 Sponge and bubble-wrap protector: Wrap an egg in a sponge and then wrap it with bubble wrap and tape.

4 Egg carton and cardboard-tube protector: Cut open a cardboard tube and cut out one section of an egg carton. Place an egg in the carton and then place in the cardboard tube. Stuff shredded tissue paper into the sides of the tube and fold the sides of the tube toward the center and seal with tape.

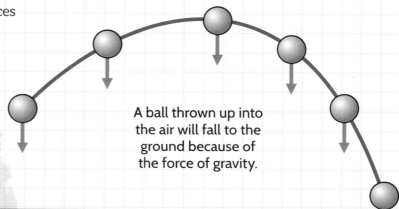

5 You can test out your eggs on one surface such as pavement, and try it out on other surfaces such as rocks, grass, or sand to see how the surface affects the landing. If you're brave you could even try dropping your creations out of a window!

SCIENCE MADE SIMPLE

When you drop the egg the force of **GRAVITY** comes into play. Gravity pulls objects toward the center of the Earth. This pulls the egg to the ground. The container that surrounds the egg acts like an airbag in a car. It protects the egg by reducing the impact felt when it hits the ground. It does this by making it collide with the ground over a slightly longer period of time which reduces the impact force. The more cushioned and protected the egg is, the less impact it feels and the less it cracks. When the egg container is about to be dropped it has energy stored in it. This energy is called **POTENTIAL ENERGY**. When the egg container has been dropped and is traveling to the ground the energy changes to **KINETIC ENERGY**, which is the energy of movement.

A ball thrown up into the air will fall to the ground because of the force of gravity.

Mini Microscope

Did you know that you can make a microscope from just a droplet of water? It might not be the most powerful magnification but it's a really fascinating way to learn about how water affects optics.

YOU WILL NEED

- ☑ Jam jar
- ☑ Plastic wrap
- ☑ A rubber band
- ☑ Water
- ☑ Specimens (see step 1)

1 Start by heading out and finding some tiny things to look at closely. These could be flowers, leaves, an insect wing, or a little bug. Choose anything that you think might look fascinating close-up.

2 Place one of your specimens in the jar. Cover with plastic wrap, pulling the wrap taut to give you a good view through the top of your jar. If you have a bug only do this for a few minutes. Add a rubber band to seal.

3 Add a droplet of water to the top of the plastic wrap and observe your specimen through the water. What happens to it? You should see that it looks bigger through the water, allowing you to look more closely at it. The water magnifies the object so that it looks roughly double its size.

SCIENCE MADE SIMPLE

The water magnifies the specimens in your jar due to something called **REFRACTION**. Refraction happens when light passes through one medium into another that has a different **DENSITY**. In this instance, the light passed from air to water. As water is denser than air, this caused the light to bend. The water droplet has a curved surface, which means it acts like a **CONVEX LENS**. This means it is thicker in the center and thinner at the edges, which causes magnification.

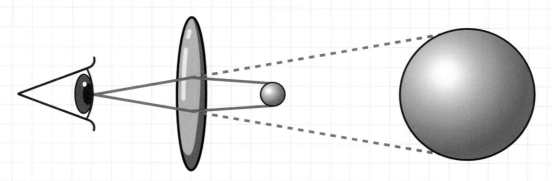

Flower Power

Learn about the different parts of a flower, and discover how to keep flowers forever by pressing them.

YOU WILL NEED
- ☑ Flowers
- ☑ Magnifying glass
- ☑ Pile of heavy books
- ☑ Paper towel
- ☑ Picture frame (optional)

SAFETY FIRST!
Note that a lot of flowers can be poisonous so make sure to wash your hands after handling them.

1 Head out to see what flowers you can find. Ask permission before pulling up anything that has been planted, and don't take too many. You only need 5–10 flowers for this project.

2 Lay out your flowers and prepare to examine them. A magnifying glass is useful to be able to see the different parts of the flower. Take one of the flowers and gently pick it apart. Can you observe the different parts listed on the right?

3 To press your flowers, open up a large book and place a sheet of paper towel on the pages. Place some flowers on top. Try to flatten the flower heads out a bit with your fingers so that the flowers will be more visible. Smaller flowers are best for this. Bulky flowers like dandelions aren't as good. Gently close the book and place a pile of heavy books on top of it. Leave for a week to flatten. After this time, open up the book to see your pressed flowers. You could then use them to make art by gluing them onto a blank card or putting them in a frame.

SCIENCE MADE SIMPLE

The parts of a flower all have an important job. The bright colors of the petals and sweet smell of the nectar serve to tempt in hungry insects, and this is when **POLLINATION** occurs. The pollen on the anther sticks to the insect as it climbs into the flower. This pollen is then transferred to the stigma—either of the same plant (**SELF-POLLINATION**) or another plant (**CROSS-POLLINATION**). Sometimes pollination happens with the wind too. The pollen then joins the female part of the flower, the ovule, and a new **SEED** is formed. Eventually, these seeds make their way back to the ground—usually by being eaten by animals, where they are digested and pooped out (in a perfect ball of fertile soil!), or carried by the wind.

Pollen is the powder on the anther that contains the male reproductive cells. The pollen sticks to insects and is carried to other plants.

The pistil is the female part of the flower containing the stigma at the top and the ovule at the bottom. The ovule matures and if it is fertilized by pollen it becomes a seed.

The petals are often colorful to attract insects.

The stamen is the male reproductive part of the flower. It consists of a filament and the anther at the top.

Sepals are the little leaves at the base of the flower that contained it as a bud.

The stem carries water and nutrients up from the soil to the leaves and flowers. This is also called a peduncle, which is a great word!

Fractal Prints

Fractals are repeating patterns that start off simple and get more and more intricate as they continue along. They are found everywhere in nature. Think of the pattern you can see in a snowflake or the way branches form on a tree—these are fractals. Have fun finding them, and turning your finds into plaster prints you can keep.

YOU WILL NEED

☑ Selection of leaves and twigs

☑ Magnifying glass (optional)

☑ About 1 cup of Plaster of Paris

☑ Pitcher

☑ Water

☑ Modeling clay

☑ Rolling pin

☑ Old silicone muffin tray

☑ Cocktail stick

☑ Round cookie cutters (to fit the muffin tray)

☑ Sandpaper

☑ Paint

1 Start by heading out and collecting leaves and twigs that show examples of fractals.

2 Have a look at your findings closely. Can you see the repeating patterns in the veins of leaves, for example, or in the fronds of a fern? Use a magnifying glass if you have one, or zoom in using a camera to see them in detail.

3 Roll out some modeling clay to about ½in (1cm) thick. Place your findings on the clay. Leave space to allow you to cut circles around the prints with your cookie cutters. Roll the rolling pin gently over the leaves to create imprints in the dough.

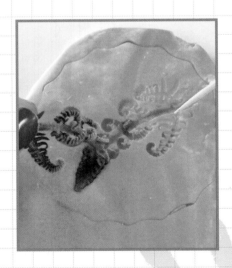

4 Use a cocktail stick to help you peel away the leaves.

5 Cut out the shapes with the cutters and press carefully, without disturbing the prints, into a muffin tray.

6 Mix up the Plaster of Paris by following the instructions on the pack. Pour into the tray and give the edges a tap to remove any bubbles. Set aside to harden for at least an hour.

7 Remove the hardened plaster from the tray and peel off the modeling clay. Any bits of clay that don't peel away can be scraped off with a cocktail stick, or left to dry out before removing.

8 Sand down the rough edges of the plaster.

9 Paint the plaster to make the patterns stand out however you would like.

SCIENCE MADE SIMPLE

Fractals occur in tiny things like the patterns on leaves and the way ice forms on a cold windowpane, up to huge things like rivers and fault lines in the earth. Even inside our bodies, our veins and lungs are made up of fractals.

Their purpose is to make things as efficient as they can be. For example, the branches of a tree split into smaller branches to help the tree get the maximum amount of light. In the same way, the roots split and repeat in order to get the most amount of **NUTRIENTS** and to hold the tree securely in the ground. You can see fractals in the way a lightning bolt strikes the ground—they work to find the quickest route to the ground.

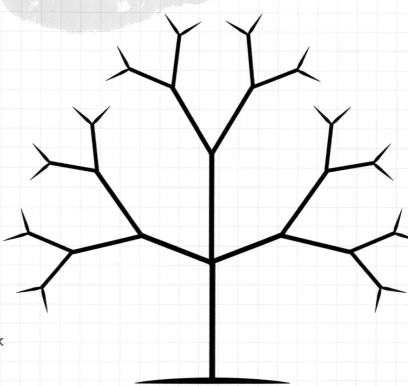

Water Clock

More than 2,000 years ago, people didn't have the luxury of looking at their watch to know the time. Clocks didn't exist! They had to come up with clever ways of measuring time. These methods included sundials (measuring the shadow of the sun), using candles, observing the stars, and using water clocks, called Clepsydras. These use the flow of water into a container to measure the passing of time.

YOU WILL NEED

- ☑ Large plastic bottle
- ☑ Awl or skewer to poke a small hole
- ☑ Marker pen
- ☑ Pitcher
- ☑ Scrap of craft foam
- ☑ Craft glue
- ☑ Stopwatch
- ☑ Scissors
- ☑ Water

1 Use sharp scissors to carefully cut the bottle in half. Take off the top.

2 With adult help poke a very small hole in the middle of the top. Put the top back. Pour water into the bottle and tip it upside down in a sink. Water should drip through the hole. If not, make the hole a little bigger.

3 Insert the top half into the bottom half of the bottle, upside down.

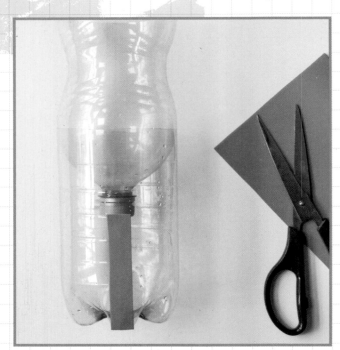

4 Cut a strip of craft foam measuring about 1in (2.5cm) wide. The height should be the measurement from the bottom of the bottle to the lid as shown. Glue it to the bottle.

5 Set up a stopwatch, pen, and pitcher of water next to the bottle. Simultaneously pour some water into the top of the bottle while starting the stopwatch.

6 Once the stopwatch reaches one minute, mark the water level on the foam strip. Keep marking each consecutive minute on the strip. Add more water to the top if it runs low.

7 One the water level has reached the bottle cap, stop the stopwatch. How many minute markers have you recorded? Add numbers to each pen mark to record the times. Pour out the water and start again. Keep an eye on the stopwatch. Does the water level match the time the second time around? Now you can use this as a timer!

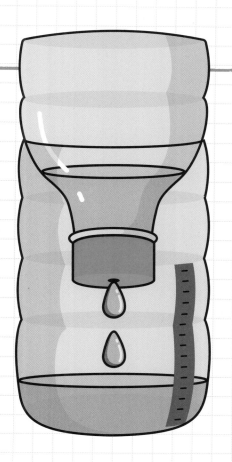

SCIENCE MADE SIMPLE

Water is predictable: The rate it flows through a hole will be the same as long as the conditions are the same. Measuring and marking the time the first time the water flowed allows us to use those marks as a time-keeping device. This works in the same way as sand timers.

Glossary

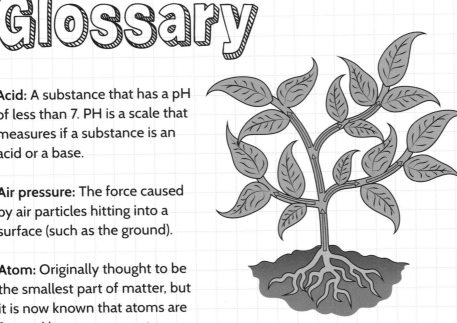

Acid: A substance that has a pH of less than 7. PH is a scale that measures if a substance is an acid or a base.

Air pressure: The force caused by air particles hitting into a surface (such as the ground).

Atom: Originally thought to be the smallest part of matter, but it is now known that atoms are formed by protons, neutrons, and electrons.

Axis: A straight line about which a body or a geometric figure rotates. For example, the Earth's axis.

Base: A substance that has a pH of greater than 7 (see Acid).

Bilateral symmetry: One-half is the mirror image of the other half.

Bubble: Air, or another gas, contained in a thin layer of liquid in a sphere.

Capillary action: The ability of a liquid to flow through narrow spaces such as tubes or sponges. This is how plants move water to their leaves.

Carbon dioxide: A colorless, odorless gas found in our atmosphere. Its chemical formula is CO_2, one carbon atom bonded to two oxygen atoms.

Chemical elements: Often referred to as simply "elements" these are substances that are only made of one type of atom. There are currently 118 elements in the periodic table.

Chemical reaction: The process of chemicals interacting and converting into other chemicals.

Condensation: The process in which a gas loses heat energy and changes into a liquid.

Constellation: A star pattern identified and named as a definite group.

Convex lens: A convex lens is thicker in the middle than it is at the edges.

Cross-linking: The joining of two or more long molecules by a bond.

Decompose: The process by which dead plants and the bodies of dead animals are slowly destroyed and broken down by natural processes.

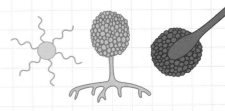

Density: A measure that shows how much mass an object has to its volume.

Diffraction: The spreading out of light waves when they meet an obstruction.

Energy: The ability to cause something around us to change, for example, moving, or heating something, or when a chemical reaction happens. Energy can be seen and stored in many different forms such as electrical, heat, or chemical.

Evaporation: The process by which liquid water becomes a vapor is called evaporation.

Force: A push or pull on an object. A force can change the movement of an object and change its speed.

Freezing point: The temperature at which a liquid becomes a solid.

Fungi: A group of living organisms that reproduce using spores and live on dead organic matter. For example, yeast, mold, and mushrooms.

Gas: A state of matter where the force between its particles is so small that it has no shape or volume.

Gravity: The force that pulls objects together. It's an invisible force that pulls everything on Earth toward the ground.

Habitat: The natural home or environment of an animal or plant.

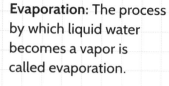

Ice crystals: Most crystals form when a liquid changes to a solid, such as when water freezes, creating ice crystals.

Kinetic Energy: The energy of movement.

Lift: A force that pushes something (like a kite) up.

Liquid: A state of matter with loosely packed particles. The particles can move but will retain their shape in a container.

Mass: The amount of matter that makes up an object.

Microorganisms: A microorganism is a living thing that is so small it must be viewed with a microscope.

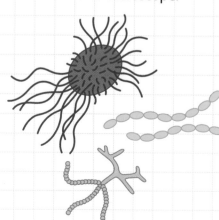

Mineral: Inorganic substances that make up Earth's rocks, sands, and soils. They are found on Earth's surface as well as deep underground.

Mold: A type of fungus. (See also Fungi).

Molecules: Atoms that are connected together with chemical bonds.

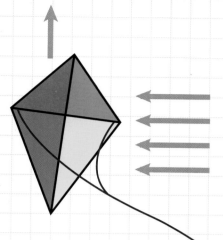

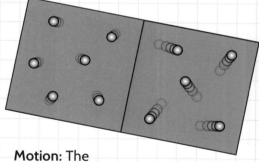

Motion: The action or process of moving or of changing place or position.

Non-Newtonian fluid: A fluid with viscosity (thickness) that varies depending on the stress or force placed on it.

Nutrient: A substance that plants or animals need in order to live and grow.

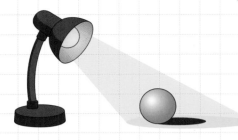

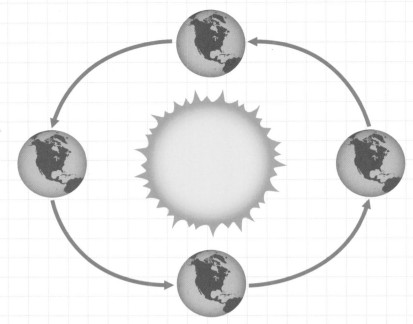

Opaque: Not able to be seen through.

Orbit: The path an object takes when it goes around something, for example, the Moon orbiting the Earth, or the Earth orbiting the Sun.

Organic: Something that comes from living plants or animals.

Organism: A living thing such as an animal or plant. Organisms need air, water, and energy to survive.

Ovule: The part of the ovary of seed plants that contains the female germ cell and after fertilization becomes the seed.

Oxygen: A colorless, odorless gas. It makes up one-fifth of the air that we breathe in.

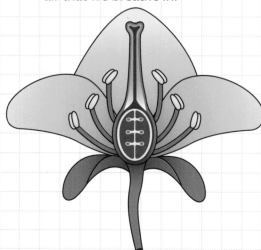

Particles: A general name for the incredibly small units that everything is made of.

Phases of the Moon: What the Moon looks like from Earth at various points, depending on how it is being lit by the Sun. There are eight phases the Moon goes through in a lunar month, which is 29.5 days long.

Photosynthesis: The process by which plants make their own food, using carbon dioxide, water, and light.

Pigments: The coloring component of paint or ink. Pigments may be in a liquid but are insoluble themselves.

Pollination: Flowering plants reproduce sexually through a process called pollination. There are two types of pollination. In self-pollination, the pollen grain lands on the same flower it originated from. In cross-pollination, the pollen grain lands on a different flower to the one it originated from.

Potential energy: The stored energy an object has as a result of its position or whether it is a solid, liquid, or gas.

Pressure: The amount of force that is acting on an area.

Radial symmetry: Symmetry around a central point instead of between sides.

Reflection: This occurs when light hits a reflective surface and bounces back at the same angle.

Reflective surface: A surface that light bounces off.

Refraction: The bending of light as it passes from one transparent substance into another.

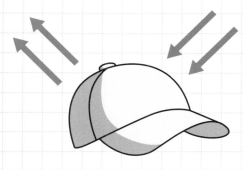

Reversible Change of State: This is when materials can be changed back to how they were before the reaction took place.

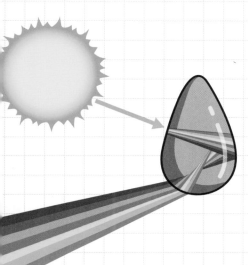

Seed: Part of a plant that can grow into a new plant. It is made up of an embryo, nutrients, and a covering called the seed coat.

Solid: A state of matter that is composed of tightly packed particles. Particles always retain their shape. (See also Liquid, Gas).

Spectrum: The range of colors that are found within light.

Sphere: A three-dimensional geometric shape, shaped like a ball.

Surface area: The amount of space covering the outside of a three-dimensional (3D) object.

Surface tension: The force that causes a layer of liquid to behave like an elastic sheet.

Symmetrical: Where two sides of something are exactly the same.

Thermal energy: Heat energy. Hotter particles have more thermal energy and will move more.

Translucent: Clear enough to allow light to pass through.

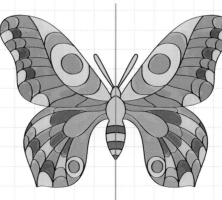

UVA and UVB rays: There are approximately 500 times more UVA rays in sunlight than UVB rays. UVA rays cause skin aging. UVB rays cause skin burning.

Volume: The space that something takes up.

Vortex: A whirling mass of air or water.

Water cycle: The path water takes as it travels within the air and Earth. It is a continuous process.

Water vapor: When it is heated, liquid water forms a gas, or vapor. The process by which liquid water becomes a vapor is called evaporation.

Wavelength: The distance between two successive crests or troughs of a wave.

Xylem: Small tubes inside a plant that draw up water.

About the Authors

Laura Minter and Tia Williams are crafters, mothers, and writers. Since starting a craft blog in 2014 they have gone on to write a large collection of books on science, crafting and creating with children. They have worked with major retailers and brands to produce craft content. Between them, they have five children who they love to make things for (and with!).

Follow them at: Instagram: @littlebuttondiaries
Tag your photos: #scienceschool

ACKNOWLEDGEMENTS

GMC Publications would like to thank our fabulous models Amelie, Lilah, Harper, Grayson, Marnie, Hema, and Amber.

First published 2024 by Button Books, an imprint of Guild of Master Craftsman Publications Ltd, Castle Place, 166 High Street, Lewes, East Sussex, BN7 1XU, UK.

ISBN 978 178708 1420

A catalog record for this book is available from the British Library.

Publisher: Jonathan Bailey
Production: Jim Bulley
Senior Project Editor: Susie Behar
Science consultant: Elinor Rose
Designer: Cathy Challinor
Main photography by Andrew Perris
Step-by-step photography by Laura Minter and Tia Williams. Illustrations on pages 5, 17, 21, 25, 33, 37, 41, 45, 55, 91, 59, 63, 73, 77, 85, 99, 103, 107, 109, 113, 117, 121, 122, 123, 124, 125 by Alex Bailey
All other illustrations from Shutterstock

Color origination by GMC Reprographics.
Printed and bound in China.

Button
Books

For more on Button Books, contact:
GMC Publications Ltd, Castle Place,
166 High Street, Lewes, East Sussex,
BN7 1XU, United Kingdom
Tel: +44 (0)1273 488005
buttonbooks.co.uk
buttonbooks.us